The Woman With Issues

Illuminations on the
Woman With the Issue of Blood

I0157120

Roosevelt Currie

CURRIE PUBLISHING COMPANY

The Scripture Quotations in The Woman With Issues Illuminations on the Woman With the Issue of Blood are from the Authorized King James Version (KJV) of the bible.

ISBN: 978-16-2550-455-5 (PB)

Brethren, I count not myself to have apprehended: but this one thing I do, forgetting those things which are behind, and reaching forth unto those things which are before, I press toward the mark for the prize of the high calling of God in Christ Jesus.

(Philippians 3:13-14)

Table of Contents

The Woman With Issues

Illuminations on the
Woman With the Issue of Blood

*A*nd a certain woman, which had an issue of blood twelve years, And had
suffered many things of many physicians,
and had spent all that she had, and was
nothing bettered, but rather grew worse,
When she had heard of Jesus, came in the
press behind, and touched his garment.
For she said, If I may touch but his
clothes, I shall be whole. And straightway
the fountain of her blood was dried up;
and she felt in her body that she was
healed of that plague. And Jesus, immediately knowing in himself that virtue had
gone out of him, turned him about in the
press, and said, Who touched my clothes?
And his disciples said unto him, Thou seest
the multitude thronging thee, and sayest
thou, Who touched me? And he looked
round about to see her that had done this
thing. But the woman fearing and trembling, knowing what was done in her,
came and fell down before him, and told

him all the truth. And he said unto her, Daughter, thy faith hath made thee whole; go in peace, and be whole of thy plague (Mark 5:25-34).

Chapter 1

Her Issues

And a certain woman, which had an issue
of blood twelve years

We would like to look at Christ's healing of issues in this discourse. There were certain events that transpired that led up to Jesus' encounter with the woman with the issue of blood.

The first healing that Saint Mark recorded in his gospel took place in the synagogue. Deliverance and healing were first needed in the church. Somebody brought an unclean spirit with them to church, and the unclean spirit could not enjoy the service with Christ in attendance. As the case would be, the unclean spirit started acting out in the presence of Christ. At least the person with the unclean spirit could get a seat in the synagogue. The woman with the issue of blood, as we will see later, couldn't get in the door.

Mark recorded, "And there was in their synagogue a man with an unclean spirit; and he cried out. Saying, Let us alone; what have we to do with thee, thou Jesus of Nazareth . . .?" (Mark 1:23-24). Please note that the man with the unclean spirit was in the synagogue when

1

Jesus got there. "And Jesus rebuked him, saying, Hold thy peace, and come out of him. And when the unclean spirit had torn him, and cried with a loud voice, he came out of him" (Mark 1:25-26). "And immediately his fame spread abroad throughout all the region round about Galilee" (Mark 1:28).

Thereafter, Jesus healed Peter's mother-in-law of a fever (Mark 1:29-31). "And at even, when the sun did set, they brought unto him all that were diseased, and them that were possessed with devils. And all the city was gathered together at the door. And he healed many that were sick of divers diseases, and cast out many devils . . ." (Mark 1:32-34).

"And he preached in their synagogues throughout all Galilee, and cast out devils. And there came a leper to him, and kneeling down to him, and saying unto him, If thou wilt, thou canst make me clean . . . And as soon as he had spoken, immediately the leprosy departed from him, and he was cleansed" (Mark 1:39-42). Jesus asked the leper not to say anything to anyone, but to go show himself to the priest and offer those things which Moses commanded (Mark 1:44). "But he went out, and began to publish it much, and to blaze abroad the matter, insomuch that Jesus could no more openly enter into the city, but was without in desert places: and they came to him from every quarter" (Mark 1:45).

And Jesus returned to Capernaum after some days, and it was noised that He was in the house (Mark 2:1). "And straightway many were gathered together, insomuch that there was no room to receive them, no, not so much as about the door: and he preached the word unto them. And they come unto him, bringing one sick of the palsy, which was borne of four" (Mark 2:2-3). Jesus forgave the man of his sins, and healed him of the palsy.

"And he entered again into the synagogue; and there was a man there which had a withered hand" (Mark 3:1). Jesus healed the man of the withered hand (Mark 3:2-5).

"But Jesus withdrew himself with his disciples to the sea: and a great multitude from Galilee followed him, and from Judea, And from Jerusalem, and from Idumaea, and from beyond Jordan; and they about Tyre and Sidon, a great multitude, when they had heard what great things he did, came unto him . . . For he had healed many; insomuch that they pressed upon him for to touch him, as many as had plagues. And unclean spirits, when they saw him, fell down before him, and cried, saying, Thou art the Son of God" (Mark 3:7-11).

"And he ordained twelve, that they should be with him, and that he might send them forth to preach, And to have power to heal sicknesses, and to cast out devils" (Mark 3:14-15).

"And the same day, when the even was come, he saith unto them, Let us pass over unto the other side . . . And there arose a great storm of wind, and the waves beat into the ship, so that it was now full . . . And he arose, and rebuked the wind, and said unto the sea, peace, be still. And the wind ceased, and there was a great calm . . . And they feared exceedingly, and said one to another, What manner of man is this, that even the wind and the sea obey him?" (Mark 4:35-41).

Thereafter, they arrived in the country of the Gadarenes. There Jesus met a man who was possessed with unclean spirits who called themselves Legion. After Jesus cast out the Legion, He told the man, ". . . Go home to thy friends, and tell them how great things the Lord hath done for thee, and hath compassion on thee. And he departed, and began to publish in Decapolis how great things Jesus had done for him: and all men did marvel" (Mark 5:19-20).

Finally, ". . . when Jesus was passed over again by ship unto the other side, much people gathered unto him: and he was nigh unto the sea. And, behold, there cometh one of the rulers of the synagogue, Jairus by name; and when he saw him, he fell at his feet, And besought him greatly, saying, My little daughter lieth at the point of death: I pray thee, come and lay thy hands on her, that she may be healed; and she shall live. And Jesus went with him; and much people followed him, and thronged him" (Mark 5:21-24). And there was in the back of the crowd, a certain woman who had an issue of blood twelve years.

This certain woman heard news of miraculous healings. This news gave her hope. She had to see for herself whether the reports were actually true. She had heard from the crowd about Jesus healing the man with the unclean spirit. She had heard about Jesus healing the man that was a paralytic. She had heard all that were diseased, and them that were possessed with devils, were healed. She had heard about a leper being healed. But most importantly, she had heard that Jesus had healed many as had plagues.

As she moved near the crowd she heard that Jairus, one of the rulers of the synagogue, had asked Jesus to accompany him back to his house to heal his daughter. So, Jesus was on the move. After hearing of Jesus this certain woman said, "If I may touch but his clothes I shall be whole." After hearing about Jesus, she believed there was hope for her. Hope is expectation with desire.

Jesus was moving in the Spirit. Jesus was moving by the Spirit. A prayer request put Him in motion! Excitement was in the air. The atmosphere was charged. Her neighborhood had responded en masse with great anticipation. Jesus was passing by where she lived. On the way to answer someone else's prayer, Jesus meets a certain woman with issues.

The atmosphere is important. Jesus was healing every condition and everybody. Jesus created this atmosphere! The expectation that folks have is important. If folks around you believe Jesus can heal, then you come to believe He can heal. If folks around you doubt and are skeptical, then you become a doubter and a skeptic. When you are in a place where folks believe God can do anything and the impossible, then that is where you come to believe God can do anything and the impossible. Faith makes all the difference. ". . . If thou canst believe, all things are possible to him that believeth" (Mark 9:23). "So then faith cometh by hearing, and hearing by the word of God" (Romans 10:17). Jesus was healing everything and everybody. "Jesus Christ the same yesterday, and today, and for ever" (Hebrews 13:8).

Women of child-bearing age typically go through a monthly menstrual cycle during which the womb builds up a lining filled with blood to nourish a child that might be conceived. This monthly menstrual cycle is also called the time of the month, the cycle, the period, her separation, or the custom of woman (Genesis 31:35). If the woman does not conceive, her body passes the blood. This is a cleansing period. In scripture, this is called "an issue of blood" (Leviticus 15:19).

The menstrual cycle can be a difficult time for some women. Sometimes a woman can experience cramps, headaches, and mood changes, and can be extremely tired because of the loss of blood.

In Leviticus 15 God told Israel that when a woman went through her separation, she was to be considered unclean, and was not to be touched by her husband. This means no sex. This separation would last seven days. If the issue of blood continued beyond seven days, then the woman herself was considered to be diseased and was to separate herself from normal human contact. "And if a woman have an issue of her blood many days out of the time of her separation, or if it run beyond the time of her separation; all the days of the issue of her uncleanness shall be as the days of her separation: she shall be unclean" (Leviticus 15:25). This woman had a condition in her life that was out of control.

7

As a result of the issue of blood this woman was considered unclean. No one could touch her and anything she touched was considered unclean (Leviticus 15:23). She was ostracized and cut off from society and excommunicated from religious observances. If she was married, she could be divorced because of her uncleanness (Deuteronomy 24:1). Worship in the synagogue would have been barred to her since she could not make atonement for her blood flow (Leviticus 15:28-30). "If the issue stops, she had to wait seven days to be declared cleansed" (Leviticus 15:28). She had been ceremonially unclean for 12 years.

This woman had a lot of things going on in her life that were of concern. She had issues. We focus generally on the fact that she had an issue of blood, but really she had other concerns too.

First, this woman had a medical issue which was diagnosed by Jesus as the plague! This woman also had financial issues. She had a history of mistreatment and abuse at the hands of many physicians. She had separation anxiety issues. She had issues of no known husband, children or relatives. She had issues of loneliness. She had issues of depression. She had issues of rejection. She was desolate, scripturally unclean, and had low self-esteem. She had no medical coverage. She was dying naturally and spiritually. And she had reached the point of desperation.

God designed this woman to be a help-meet, but before she could get to that, she had to deal with her issues. For the woman with issues, there is a need for Jesus. All this woman had to look forward to was suffering and menopause. But menopause brings with it a whole new set of issues. This woman had suffered in this condition and with these issues for 12 years.

Chapter 2

Her Suffering

And she had suffered many things of many physicians, and had spent all that she had, and was nothing bettered, but rather grew worse

One of the key things about this woman was that she suffered. There are many women today that are suffering and suffering in silence. This woman consulted and was treated by many doctors and advice givers. She had endured medical treatments at a substantial cost. She had suffered as a result of these medical treatments and home remedies. They all came up short and it appeared she was hopelessly incurable. She had only grown worse under the doctors' care. She had literally tried everything.

She suffered within and without. This woman's suffering affected her greatly. Suffering can purify and change you. It can strip away all the things that are not important and cause us to re-evaluate what's really important in our lives. You can learn a lot through suffering. "For it became him, for whom are all things, and by whom are all things, in bringing many sons unto glory, to make the captain of their salvation perfect through sufferings (Hebrews 2:10).

This woman could live without the blood, so to speak, and without the money, but the loneliness, isolation and spiritual death she experienced day after day caused her to suffer beyond words imaginable. It was God who said, ". . . It is not good that the man should be alone . . ." (Genesis 2:18). This woman suffered as a result of her condition, the treatment of the condition, and the aftereffects of the condition.

Every day for 12 straight years this woman suffered. For 12 years straight this woman was cut off from the presence of God. She could not go to the synagogue, Sabbath services, Passover, feasts, or ceremonies. For 12 years she was unclean and untouchable. For 12 years she had no television, telephone, radio, or the internet for companionship or entertainment. For 12 years she could not receive hugs, kisses, back rubs, embraces, or any type of romantic affection. For 12 years she did not have any sexual relations, which could possibly have added to her frustrations. She was the walking dead. She was a social outcast. She was completely cut off from family, friends, and society. She had nobody to talk to or talk with. She couldn't hang out at the well with the other women (John 4:5-7). And she couldn't go shopping for sandals at the local bazaar.

There are a lot of women that live lives that are all alone. They go to their job, go shopping, go to restaurants, visit friends, have pets, work around the house and in the garden, and attend church on a daily and weekly basis but yet are all alone. They have children, family, and careers, but they are all alone. They live and work in the midst of people but they are all alone. When you want to punish someone in jail or prison you put them in solitary confinement; sometimes with children you tell them to go to their room, or stand in a corner. The time out and separation is meant to be punishment.

It is possible to be alone and not be lonely. However, you can be in a midst of a crowd and be all alone. You can be in the midst of a crowd and be out of touch. There are a lot of women that live lives in quiet desperation.

There was no outward evidence or visible manifestation of what was going on physically with her. You could not look at her and tell she suffered inwardly. There are people like that today. Like this woman, you have things going on with you that are not readily seen or apparent. You have things of concern. Some things are just the tip of the iceberg. There are more dangerous things going on underneath, that will sink folks that come too close. There is no telling what lies beneath the surface. You couldn't look at this woman and tell she had issues.

You can have issues and not suffer, but this woman had issues and suffered and grew worse. There are some folks that have issues and are suffering, but you would never know it. You couldn't tell by looking at them that their whole life is falling apart. They accept their situation as part of life. They accept their condition as the will of God.

There was a famine in Israel, and God told Elijah the Tishbite, "Arise, get thee to Zarephath, which belongeth to Sidon, and dwell there: behold, I have commanded a widow woman there to sustain thee (1 Kings 17:9). ". . . many widows were in Israel in the days of Elijah, when the heaven was shut up three years and six months, when great famine was throughout all the land; But unto none of them was Elijah sent, save unto Sarepta, a city of Sidon, unto a woman that was a widow (Luke 4:25-26). This woman was suffering, and had spent all she had, and things were getting worse. When the woman met Elijah, she said, ". . . As the Lord thy God liveth, I have not a cake, but a handful of meal in a barrel, and a little oil in a cruse: and, behold, I am gathering two sticks, that I may go in and dress it for me and my son, that we may eat it, and die (1 Kings 17:12). This woman had an external condition in her life that was draining her of everything she had. Things had dried up. She and her son were suffering and dying. She felt she was at the end of her road and could see no relief. She had got down to almost nothing, and she thought it was the end. But unbeknownst to her help was on the way. Beloved, God knows you're suffering. God knows where you are, and help is on the way!

This woman with the issue of blood spent all that she had; which included time, energy, and money. The scriptures state, ". . . money is a defense . . ." (Ecclesiastes 7:12). This woman had no money and therefore no defense. She was defenseless. She had no protection.

Think of all the issues that have come up in your life that could have been resolved, if you just had the money. There are a lot of issues that can be resolved with money. The scriptures state, ". . . money answereth all things" (Ecclesiastes 10:19).

Most women understand it takes money to survive, when it comes to everyday life. This woman with the issue of blood found herself in a place where she could not answer her creditors and had no defense. When the money ran out so did her treatment. When the money ran out so did her options. Her condition drained her of everything. There are a lot of issues that can drain you of all your resources. Your resources can be exhausted as a result of a medical condition, drug or alcohol addiction, children's needs, gambling, divorce, unemployment, bad investments, impulse spending or shopping, or a man!

There are things you can live with and things you can live without. Some women can't live without a certain purse or designer outfit. Some women can't live without a husband, even if it is somebody else's husband (John 4:16-18).

By the same token there are some issues you can't live with. They set you off; they push you over the edge; there are some things you have a problem with. There are some things you can't shout over or dance around. Some things you need deliverance from. Out of sheer desperation some folks will try anything, and take all kinds of chances in order to get out of certain situations.

How many women are looking for something or someone to make their life better? Some women are only looking for a Boaz. Some are looking for that something that they think will make them whole or complete. However, the scriptures state, "For in him dwelleth all the fullness of the Godhead bodily. And ye are complete in him . . ." (Colossians 2:9-10). Some of us are in a lot of stuff, but it's not Jesus. What this woman really needed, was to be in Jesus—Jesus is still the answer today! You are complete in Him!

After spending all of her resources and not getting any better, the bible says she grew worse! Her condition did not get better. Doctors upon examination of a patient typically look for symptoms. The purpose is to make an accurate diagnosis. The diagnosis is important for the treatment. The wrong diagnosis will lead to the wrong treatment. You have to really know what you are dealing with. This woman had a medical condition that was described as an issue of blood, fountain of her blood, and the plague.

This woman and her condition grew worse. She didn't just get worse. She grew worse. That means her condition started out small and progressively changed and didn't get better with time. You can assume that she had a life before the 12 year period of this condition. There was a time when she had plenty of money and no serious condition. But she developed a condition and it took complete control of her life. As with this woman, most things have a beginning.

The problem started with her blood. She was losing blood, losing her life, and slowly losing her mind. "For the life of the flesh is in the blood . . ." (Leviticus 17:11). She was dying a slow death.

There are people yet dying in your midst. They are slowly dying in an unhappy relationship. They are dying from smoking, drug and alcohol addictions, work related stress, poor diet or overeating. People are dying both naturally and spiritually.

For this woman, every year her condition got worse. After every treatment it got worse. At one point it was just a trickle of blood. Then it became an issue of blood! Sometimes we see a trickle and decide to wait. You think it's probably nothing. You don't want to sound the alarm. You're so busy with other folk's issues and decide to deal with yours later. But there was a woman in the Song of Solomon who said, ". . . they made me the keeper of the vineyards; but mine own vineyard have I not kept" (Song of Solomon 1:6).

You can't wait until it's too late! Some things you need to deal with early. Nobody can take care of your vineyard like you. Sometimes you are appointed to a certain office or position in the church. This is wonderful. But sometimes the duties of the office or position require you to sacrifice yourself at the expense of your husband, family, and home!

This woman had this condition for 12 years. The 12 years represent a season in this woman's life. The 12 years represented a period of time.

In the book of Ecclesiastes it states, "To every thing there is a season, and a time to every purpose under the heaven: A time to be born, and a time to die; a time to plant, and a time to pluck up that which is planted; A time to kill, and a time to heal; a time to break down, and a time to build up; A time to weep, and a time to laugh; a time to mourn, and a time to dance; A time to cast away stones, and a time to gather stones together; a time to embrace, and a time to refrain from embracing; A time to get, and a time to lose; a time to keep, and a time to cast away; A time to rend, and a time to sew; a time to keep silence, and a time to speak; A time to love, and a time to hate; a time of war, and a time of peace" (Ecclesiastes 3:1-8).

We need to know where we are in the season of things. God said, "While the earth remaineth, seedtime and harvest, and cold and heat, and summer and winter, and day and night shall not cease (Genesis 8:22). You have to figure out where you are in the season of things.

The scriptures state, "To every thing there is a season." In this list of opposites there was a season of good and a season of bad. There is a season of sowing and a season of reaping. These are issues you can look forward to. Life is all about balance. The issues in your life will balance out in time. You will have days with and days without. These are times when you can get pretty emotional. I believe this woman was going through all of these emotions.

This woman was going through a season of losing. This was a time in her life to lose. This was a time to break down. This woman was losing blood on a daily basis. She had lost her health, wealth, husband, and friends. But soon it would be a time to get. It would be a time to receive. Soon it would be a time to laugh, dance, embrace, and love. Soon it would be a time of healing. The same is equally applicable to you. Whatever is going on in your life is just for a season, for a period of time. Even with Jesus we find, "And when the devil had ended all the temptation, he departed from him for a season" (Luke 4:13). ". . . weeping may endure for a night [season], but joy cometh in the morning" (Psalm 30:5).

Sometimes during a routine checkup the doctor notices something is not quite right. They need to do more tests. They tell you not to worry. It started out as a little pain or a little lump. Then you're told that little pain or lump is terminal cancer. After that everything changes.

What did David mean when he said, "O God, thou art my God; early will I seek thee . . ." (Psalm 63:1)? It means to seek God early in the morning in prayer, but it also means to seek God early in your situation. You shouldn't start seeking God when there is nothing else left or no one else to turn to.

You should seek God before there is a full blown crisis. The disciples waited until things were out of control before they went to Jesus. The disciples waited until their ship was full of water before they woke up Jesus. It wasn't the wind or the waves that woke up Jesus. Jesus was asleep on a pillow. The disciples woke Him up.

Most folks will find themselves awakened when their faith is asleep. But when your faith is awake, then you can sleep. While the disciples were trying to deal with the water and stressing out, things got progressively worse (Mark 4:35-41). While the storm raged, the disciples began to be filled with concern, anxiety, frustration, and fear. While they were being filled with these emotions, the ship filled with water. When the disciples took on concern the ship went a little lower in the water. When the disciples took on anxiety and frustration the ship sank lower. As fear filled their hearts, they began to sink deeper and deeper until they reached a point of complete panic.

The disciples were experienced fishermen. They tried to handle the ship as the storm developed. They thought they had everything under control. They were used to storms by virtue of their occupation. However, this storm scared them. Some storms can turn into, ". . . a tempestuous wind, called Euroclydon" (Acts 27:14). Sometimes it just takes minutes for some things to get completely out of control. Then the disciples remembered Jesus. Then they began to look to Him. However, He was there with them all the time. Problems are the things you see when you take your eyes off Jesus. The disciples hurried to wake Him up. However, they should have went to Jesus in prayer when they first felt the wind blow. "Be careful for nothing; but in every thing by prayer and supplication with thanksgiving let your requests be made known unto God. And the peace of God, which passeth all understanding, shall keep your hearts and minds through Christ Jesus" (Philippians 4:6-7).You need to seek God early in your situation!

In the book of Psalms it states, "They that go down to the sea in ships, that do business in great waters; These see the works of the Lord, and his wonders in the deep. For he commandeth, and raiseth the stormy wind, which lifteth up the waves thereof. They mount up to the heaven, they go down again to the depths: their soul is melted because of you. They reel to and fro, and stagger like a drunken man, and are at their wit's end. Then they cry unto the Lord in their trouble, and he bringeth them out of their distresses. He maketh the storm a calm, so that the waves thereof are still. Then are they glad because they be quiet; so he bringeth them unto their desired haven. Oh that men would praise the Lord for his goodness, and for his wonderful works to the children of men! Let them exalt him also in the congregation of the people, and praise him in the assembly of the elders" (Psalm 107:23-32).

Have you ever been at wit's end? It wasn't until these mariners were at their wit's end that they called on the Lord. The bible states, "Then they cry unto the Lord in their trouble, and he bringeth them out of their distresses" The scriptures state in the book of Malachi, "For I am the Lord, I change not; therefore ye sons of Jacob are not consumed" (Malachi 3:6). "Jesus Christ the same yesterday, and today, and for ever" (Hebrews 13:8). You really need to seek God early in prayer! The Lord can bring you out.

The disciples were concerned about the water and drowning. They were worried about the symptoms. Jesus rebuked the wind and told the sea, peace be still. Then the water wasn't an issue. We need to deal with the root of the problem. You can trim or cut back a plant, but if the root is intact it will continually grow back. And if left unaddressed it will take over your whole garden. The root of a lot of problems is sin. The symptoms are smoking, drinking, lying, cursing, and a hundred thousand other things, but the root is sin. If you get rid of sin, if you get rid of the root, the symptoms will also go away. We need to deal with the root of our issues.

This woman had been bleeding for 12 years. She spent all her money on doctors. Perhaps she didn't go to the priest because of what she had heard happened to that certain man in the parable of the Good Samaritan or maybe she met the Priest and Levite and they passed her by too. She wasn't stripped of her raiment, wounded, and left half dead, but she had the plague. Sometimes that's all folks need to know to give them a reason to pass you by. But some women don't need a reason not to like you; they just don't.

Sometimes we can't tell by looking at you whether you've got the plague. But folks will pass you by when you look; dress, smell, and talk like you have the plague. Folks won't have time for you. They've got their own issues.

Beloved, do you have any medical, economic, social, emotional or psychological issues? It is within your ability and responsibility to take care of yourself. Press your way into the presence of God! The Lord won't pass you by.

In spite of all of her sufferings, this woman was determined to see Jesus. This woman was determined to touch Jesus. This woman was determined to be healed. She was losing her blood, slowly losing her life, but she was holding on.

Chapter 3

Her Determination

When she had heard of Jesus, she came in the press behind, and touched his garment. For she said, If I may touch but his clothes, I shall be · whole. And straightway the fountain of her blood was dried up; and she felt in her body that she was healed of that plague

This woman heard that Jesus was healing, and that He had healed other folks of the plague. And she thought, "that's where I am. That's the street I live on. That's what's going on in my life." She believed Jesus could do the same for her. If only she could just get to Him. Right now Jesus was actually passing by! It's interesting that Jesus was the last place she looked. Jesus should have been the first place to look. Only He can deliver you from your condition. Only He can bring you out.

This woman heard of Jesus healing and believed it to be true. Then she heard He was passing by! She began searching for the Way, the Truth, and the Life (John 14:6). She started out following the crowd. She started out behind, in the back. She had never seen Jesus before, and didn't know what He looked like, but she believed He could heal her. And she was determined to find Him. She was determined to risk it all. She was determined to get help for herself. All that mattered was that she touched Him. She was a woman on a mission. She was a woman obsessed.

It's that journey into the presence of the Lord that we're having some difficulty with. This is both an inward and outward journey. It starts first within, "For she said within herself, if I may but touch his garment, I shall be whole" (Matthew 9:21).

The first thing required in following or seeking the Lord is hearing the word, then obedience. Jesus told the disciples, ". . . Follow me, and I will make you fishers of men. And they straightway left their nets, and followed him" (Matthew 4:19-20).

The disciples at this point had little or no faith. They heard the word. Then they obeyed the word and faith came later. "So then faith cometh by hearing, and hearing by the word of God" (Romans 10:17). Faith is a requirement to receiving from God. "But without faith it is impossible to please him: for he that cometh to God must believe that he is, and that he is a rewarder of them that diligently seek him" (Hebrew11:6). Jesus said, ". . . If thou canst believe, all things are possible to him that believeth" (Mark 9:23).

Prayer is the vehicle or tool that God has left for us to use to get in touch with Him. Prayer is the vehicle that you can get in to take you into the presence of God. Prayer is the tool that you can use to gain entrance into the presence of God.

Prayer is what you use to bring you into the presence of God. In God's presence is where all of your needs can be met! David said, ". . . in thy presence is fullness of joy; at thy right hand there are pleasures forevermore" (Psalms 16:11). Throughout the whole New Testament we see folks pressing their way into the presence of Jesus, and they were not disappointed.

This woman pressed her way into the presence of God. This woman was determined. This is where we lose out and things get complicated. Jesus is not here physically. He's on the right hand of God making intercession for us. But you can still reach out and touch Him through praise and thanksgiving as He is passing by through His Spirit.

You can press your way into the presence of God. You can reach this state by blocking out everything in your mind but feelings of happiness and joy. The scriptures declare, ". . .

whatsoever things are true, whatsoever things are honest, whatsoever things are just, whatsoever things are pure, whatsoever things are lovely, whatsoever things are of good report; if there be any virtue, and if there be any praise, think on these things" (Philippians 4:8). As you are thinking on God's goodness, close your eyes and focus on the Lord, and say "thank you Jesus" "thank you Lord" over and over again. Rejoice and be exceedingly glad. Don't stop until you are in the presence of God. The Lord will fill you with love, peace, and joy!

David said in the book of Psalms, "Thus will I bless thee while I live: I will lift up my hands in thy name (Psalm 63:4). "Lift up your hands in the sanctuary, and bless the Lord (Psalm 134:2). And in the New Testament, "I will therefore that men pray everywhere, lifting up holy hands, without wrath and doubting (1Timothy 2:8). When you hold up your hands and arms in prayer, you're asking God to lift you. You're asking God to pick you up. Your hands and arms are spiritual antennas. The higher the antenna is raised, the better the reception.

The Apostle Paul remembered a time when he was raising his antennas. Paul said, "I knew a man in Christ above fourteen years ago, (whether in the body, I cannot tell; or whether out of the body, I cannot tell: God knoweth;) such a one caught up to the third heaven. And I knew such a man, (whether in the body, or out of the body, I cannot tell: God knoweth;) How that he was caught up into paradise, and heard unspeakable words, which it is not lawful for a man to utter (2 Corinthians 12:2-4). "Therefore we are always confident, knowing that, whilst we are at home in the body, we are absent from the Lord . . . We are confident, I say, and willing rather to be absent from the body, and to be present with the Lord (2 Corinthians 5:6-8).

It is so important to understand Christ's teaching on pressing into the presence of God. There was a man that was in sin and he was sick of the palsy. He had four friends who decided to take him into the presence of God. They made it their mission. They were determined. And the scriptures declare, "And straightway many were gathered together, insomuch that there was no room to receive them, no, not so much as about the door: and he preached the word unto them. And they come unto him, bringing one sick of the palsy, which was borne of four. And when they could not come nigh unto him for the press, they uncovered the roof where he was: and when they had broken it up, they let down the bed wherein the sick of the palsy lay. When Jesus saw their faith, he said unto the sick of the palsy, Son, thy sins be forgiven thee" (Mark 2:2-5).

These men were trying to gain access into the presence of God. When they got to the house they could not come nigh to Jesus for the press. They found themselves at the back of the crowd. They went all around the house, but they couldn't get through the doors or windows. That's when they looked up and knew what they had to do! Sometimes you just need to look up! David said, "I will lift up mine eyes unto the hills, from whence cometh my help. My help cometh from the Lord, which made heaven and earth" (Psalm 121:1-2). Sometimes you have to ask for help when you're seeking help. Sometimes you need help while you're looking for help. These four men were carrying this man in his bed. All five men worked together. When they got to the side of the house they scaled the walls and hoisted the paralytic to the roof. When they made it on top there was still no clear way to Jesus. At that point they uncovered the roof and broke it up with their bare hands. Then they set themselves and lowered the man in his bed into the presence of Christ. God wants you to see how these men went around, over, under and through to get to Jesus! We see determination! We see endurance!

These men pressed their way into the presence of God and were able to receive what their friend needed from the Lord. They had the faith and faith made a way. Their key to victory was endurance. The key to this woman's survival was endurance. Some things you have to endure. You have to press your way. The same endurance she used to survive 12 years, she used the same endurance to reach Jesus.

Beloved, you have to be determined. Then you have to endure. You may be in the beginning, middle, or end of your season, and God's message to you is—endure! Press your way. ". . . Be thou faithful unto death . . ." (Revelation 2:10). Paul told Timothy to, "endure hardness, as a good soldier of Jesus Christ" (2 Timothy 2:3), and to "endure afflictions" (2 Timothy 4:5). We are told to look, ". . . unto Jesus the author and finisher of our faith; who for the joy that was set before him endured the cross, despising the shame, and is set down at the right hand of the throne of God" (Hebrews 12:2). God would have you endure till the end of your season. ". . . he that endureth to the end shall be saved" (Matthew 10:22). Be patient. For, "In your patience possess ye your souls" (Luke 21:19).

You need to first pray into the presence of God, then that's when you should— "Ask, and it shall be given you; seek, and ye shall find; knock, and it shall be opened unto you: For every one that asketh receiveth; and he that seeketh findeth; and to him that knocketh it shall be opened" (Matthew 7:7-8).

When it came to prayer, Jesus said, ". . . my house shall be called the house of prayer . . ." (Matthew 21:13). This means the church, but also this is speaking of your physical house. This is speaking of your body. And prayer should be going on all the time. The church should be a praying church. God said, "Rejoice evermore. Pray without ceasing. In every thing give thanks: for this is the will of God in Christ Jesus concerning you" (1 Thessalonians 5:16-18). God meant for us to pray. Jesus told His disciples, "And when thou prayest . . ." (Matthew 6:5). Not if, but when. Jesus referenced prayer four times in the sixth chapter of Matthew, "And when thou prayest . . . But thou, when thou prayest . . . But when ye pray . . . After this manner therefore pray ye . . ." (Matthew 6:5-9). Jesus said, ". . . men ought always to pray, and not to faint" (Luke 18:1).

Paul said, "I exhort therefore, that, first of all, supplications, prayers, intercessions, and giving of thanks, be made for all men" (1 Timothy 2:1). When it came to prayer, we find Peter and John going to the temple at the hour of prayer (Acts 3:1). Later we see the disciples declare in response to an issue in the church, "But we will give ourselves continually to prayer, and to ministry of the word" (Acts 6:4). The disciples were determined to give themselves continually to prayer. Prayer should be the first thing in your life. Prayer should be your number one priority.

God has things for you that can only be received through prayer. Of all the places you can be, there is a place you need to be. You need to take your issues into the presence of God. David said, ". . . in thy presence is fullness of joy; at thy right hand there are pleasures forevermore" (Psalms 16:11). You should seek to dwell in the presence of God. If the truth be told, you need the fullness of joy. You need the pleasures for evermore. You should seek to enter and dwell in the presence of God.

In the Old Testament, Elijah told King Ahab, ". . . As the Lord God of Israel liveth, before whom I stand . . ." (1 Kings 17:1). And in the New Testament the scriptures state, "And the angel answering said unto him, I am Gabriel, that stand in the presence of God . . ." (Luke 1:19). The secret of their success and power can be found in that they lived and dwelled in the presence of God. It's a blessing to come before and to continually dwell in His presence. Whatever you are in the presence of is what you will become. This is true both naturally and spiritually.

On the natural side, whatever you let into your presence is what you will become. The music and the entertainment of this world will affect you. It will get into your mind, heart, and spirit. "For as he thinketh in his heart, so is he . . ." (Proverbs 23:7). A man's character is the sum total of all his thoughts. If he watches and thinks negative and violent things, then he will be negative and violent. "As he thinketh in his heart, so is he . . ." Therefore, "Keep thy heart with all diligence; for out of it are the issues of life" (Proverbs 4:23). "And he said, That which cometh out of the man, that defileth the man. For from within, out of the heart of men, proceed evil thoughts, adulteries, fornications, murders, Thefts, covetousness, wickedness, deceit, lasciviousness, an evil eye, blasphemy, pride, foolishness: All these evil things come from within, and defile the man" (Mark7:20-23).

Your mind and heart is like a garden. Whatever you put in, is what is going to come out. Whatever you plant or allow in your heart will grow and bring forth fruit. If you plant a kernel of corn in your natural garden, and water it, it will yield a stalk with at least 4-6 ears of corn. We understand this in the natural, but don't fully understand this in the spiritual. The law is the same on both the natural and spiritual level. "Be not deceived; God is not mocked: for whatsoever a man soweth, that shall he also reap. For he that soweth to his flesh shall of the flesh reap corruption; but he that soweth to the Spirit shall of the Spirit reap life everlasting" (Galatians 6:7-8).

You can see the effects of dwelling in the Lord's presence on the spiritual side in the life of Moses: "And he [Moses] was there with the Lord forty days and forty nights; he did neither eat bread, nor drink water. And he wrote upon the tablets the words of the covenant, the ten commandments. And it came to pass, when Moses came down from mount Sinai with the two tablets of testimony in Moses' hand, that Moses wist not that the skin of his face shone while he talked with them" (Exodus 34:28-29). Being in the presence of God changed Moses! "Now the Lord is that Spirit: and where the Spirit of the Lord is, there is liberty. But we all, with open face beholding as in a glass the glory of the Lord, are changed into the same image from glory to glory, even as by the Spirit of the Lord" (2 Corinthians 3:17-18).

This woman got into the press, physically. There are people that come out just to see. Some folks are drawn by the crowd. Some folks are just spectators. When the town folks of Decapolis heard about what happened to the man with the Legion, ". . . they went out to see what it was that was done" (Mark 5:14).

But this woman had a need. This woman was determined. Today you need to get into the press and don't worry about the rest. The key is focus. The key is to look to Jesus. "If I may touch but His clothes, I shall be whole." Jesus is the object of our faith. We miss that! We need to get through to Jesus. You can sit right in your living room and get through to Jesus. This is how you do it. You have to focus, concentrate, believe, pray, and press your way. This was her formula for victory. This should be your formula for victory. Let us examine what she did. She went to where Jesus was moving. She hoped. She expected. She believed. She received. It will still work today. God hasn't changed, has He? OK, then the problem is you. You need to find your way to where Jesus is presently working and moving, because He is the same yesterday, today, and forever.

This certain woman could not go directly to Jesus like Jairus because of her condition. She thought to sneak up behind Him. She thought to hide in the crowd. This certain woman had to sneak through the crowd. Now you don't have to sneak upon Jesus because of your condition. We are told in the scriptures, "Let us therefore come boldly unto the throne of grace, that we may obtain mercy, and find grace to help in time of need" (Hebrews 4:16).

This woman needed healing. This woman decided, ". . . this one thing I do, forgetting those things which are behind, and reaching forth unto those things which are before, I press toward the mark . . ." (Philippians 3:13-14). There are all kinds of healing, and she was looking for all of it. She was "Looking unto Jesus the author and finisher of our faith . . ." (Hebrew 12:2). Again, "Jesus Christ the same yesterday, and today, and for ever" (Hebrews 13:8). There is mercy and grace waiting for you. "And God is able to make all grace abound toward you . . ." (2 Corinthians 9:8).

Don't let the crowd stop you from seeing Jesus. You need to see Jesus. This woman didn't have just a need, but a desperate need. For every issue or question, the answer is always the same—Jesus!

Jesus can heal your finances, broken heart, loneliness, depression, and body of whatever condition you have. Jesus can heal even cancer.

"When the wicked, even mine enemies and my foes, came upon me to eat up my flesh, they stumbled and fell" (Psalm 27:2). Jesus is the answer to cancer. Jesus can put a stop to the things that are running out of control in your life.

For some, their spending, eating, drinking, and sex life is out of control. For some, their flesh is out of control. "Is there anything too hard for the Lord . . .?" (Genesis 18:14). The answer is absolutely not! "Now unto him that is able to do exceeding abundantly above all that we ask or think, according to the power that worketh in us" (Ephesians 3:20).

"And straightway the fountain of her blood was dried up." Mark describes in graphic terms this woman's condition. She had within her a fountain of blood that manifested itself in a continuous flow. This fountain flowed on a continuous basis. It was a condition she had no control over. It leaked like a faucet with a bad washer. It ran like a river. However, this fountain of blood was dried up by the Son! "But unto you that fear my name shall the Sun of righteousness arise with healing in his wings . . ." (Malachi 4:2). And God can dry up every stream, pool, river, aquaphor, reservoir, ocean, or seas of conditions in your life. "For we have heard how the Lord dried up the water of the

Red sea for you . . ." (Joshua 2:10). God literally can dry up the Red Sea! "Behold, I am the Lord, the God of all flesh: is there any thing too hard for me?" (Jeremiah 32:27).

"And she felt in her body that she was healed of that plague." There was not a moment of hesitation in His actions. That is the way He answers our prayers still today. The scripture states, "And there came a leper to him, and kneeling down to him, and saying unto him, If thou wilt, thou canst make me clean. And Jesus, moved with compassion, put forth his hand, and touched him, and saith unto him, I will; be thou clean. And as soon as he had spoken, immediately the leprosy departed from him, and he was cleansed" (Mark 1:40-42). If you call on Him, He will answer prayer! Jesus can put a stop to anything. Jesus can heal any condition! "And Jesus came and spake unto them, saying, All power is given unto me in heaven and in earth" (Matthew 28:18). "For in him dwelleth all the fullness of the Godhead bodily" (Colossians 2:9). Just consider, Jesus has all power. And in Him dwelleth all the fullness of the Godhead bodily. And you are a part of Him by being a member of the church, His body. All of God's power and fullness is available to you right now!

In answer to the prayer of Joshua, the Lord stopped the sun and the moon for a whole day. "Then spake Joshua to the Lord in the day when the Lord delivered up the Amorites before the children of Israel, Sun, stand thou still upon Gibeon; and thou Moon, in the valley of Ajalon. And the Sun stood still, and the Moon stayed, until the people had avenged themselves upon their enemies. Is not this written in the book of Jasher? So the sun stood still in the midst of heaven, and hasted not to go down about a whole day" (Joshua 10:12-13). There is nothing God can't do for you!

In answer to prayer Elijah took the key out of his pocket and turned off the water in Israel for three years and six months. Being one with God made Elijah the majority, not the minority. "Elijah was a man subject to like passions as we are, and he prayed earnestly that it might not rain: and it rained not on the earth by the space of three years and six months. And he prayed again, and the heaven gave rain, and the earth brought forth her fruit" (James 5:17-18). There is nothing God won't do for you!

While Hezekiah was King of Jerusalem, he was attacked by the king of Assyria. The city was surrounded by 185,000 Assyrians. Each one of these men individually could have killed Hezekiah. Each one of these men was an issue for Hezekiah. "And it came to pass that night, that the angel of the Lord went out, and smote in the camp of the Assyrians an hundred fourscore and five thousand: and when they arose early in the morning, behold, they were all dead corpses" (2 Kings 19:35). In answer to prayer, God delivered Hezekiah out of 185,000 issues overnight! When you count your issues, I doubt they number 185,000. Beloved, there is no limit to what God will do for you!

Jesus did not heal everyone that touched Him in the crowd. Jesus felt the hand of faith. This woman drew out of Him what she needed. Jesus perceived her secret touch. Jesus healed her body by His power immediately and completely as a result of her touch.

This woman had a secret. She didn't want folks around her in the crowd to know. Sometimes we have issues that are personal and embarrassing that we would like to keep secret. Some folks have unspoken prayer requests for whatever reasons. Sometimes you don't want the pastor and the church to know. Some things you just want between you and God. Christ allowed her to be healed in secret, but He couldn't let her slip away in the crowd. She believed simply touching His clothes would heal her. Because she was willing to touch Jesus, she was healed.

Chapter 4

Her Touch

And Jesus, immediately knowing in himself that virtue had gone out of him, turned him about in the press, and said, Who touched my clothes? And his disciples said unto him, Thou seest the multitude thronging thee, and sayest thou, Who touched me? And he looked round about to see her that had done this thing.

The healing of this certain woman cost Jesus. Virtue (power) flowed out from Jesus into the woman. Jesus felt virtue drain from His body. In another scripture it states, "And the whole multitude sought to touch him: for there went virtue out of him, and healed them all" (Luke 6:19). We need to let the virtue in! When the Lord enters the temple, He fixes everything that needs fixing, and then provides the healing that's needed. "And Jesus went into the temple of God, and cast out all them that sold and bought in the temple, and overthrew the tables of the moneychangers, and the seats of them that sold doves. And said unto them, It is written, My house shall be called the house of prayer; but ye have made it a den of thieves. And the blind and the lame came to him in the temple;

and he healed them" (Matthew 21:12-14). Jesus went into the temple and everything that wasn't right had to leave. Then the blind and the lame came to him in the temple; and he healed them. Beloved, let Him in! All you need to do to let Him in is to say yes! Yes Lord! Jesus said, "Behold, I stand at the door, and knock: if any man hear my voice, and open the door, I will come in to him, and will sup with him, and he with me" (Revelation 3:20). Let Him in!

The disciples were unaware of what it cost Jesus to minister. They were not aware of the virtue when it left. This was brought to our attention for our benefit. This was for our edification. "Who also hath made us able ministers of the new testament; not of the letter, but of the spirit: for the letter killeth, but spirit giveth life" (2 Corinthians 3:6). "He therefore that ministereth to you the Spirit, and worketh miracles among you, doeth he it by the works of the law, or by the hearing of faith?" (Galatians 3:5). In the book of Zechariah it states, "Then he answered and spake unto me, saying, This is the word of the Lord unto Zerubbabel, saying, Not by might, not by power, but by my spirit, saith the Lord of hosts" (Zechariah 4:6).

How and when did Jesus receive this virtue? At the beginning of His ministry Jesus was filled with the Holy Ghost (Matthew 3:16). "Then was Jesus led up of the Spirit into the wilderness to be tempted of the devil. And when he had fasted forty days and forty nights, he was afterward an hungered" (Matthew 4:1-2). "And when the devil had ended all the temptation, he departed from him for a season. And Jesus returned in the power of the Spirit into Galilee . . ." (Luke 4:13-14). This virtue, power, and anointing is cultivated and kept by fasting and prayer. We have to follow the example of the Master. We need a forty!

Jesus ministered the Spirit, and we're called to minister the Spirit. ". . . we have this treasure in earthen vessels . . ." (2 Corinthians 4:7). ". . . the anointing which ye have received of him abideth in you . . ." (1 John 2:27). When you touch folks, and when they touch you, they should be helped. It's because of the virtue, power, and anointing within you! It's because of the anointing upon you!

The disciples were surprised at Jesus' question: "Who touched me?" He was completely surrounded by a mass of people. It would be better to ask who hadn't touched Him. How could He possibly expect not to be touched? Many touched and bumped, but only one touched by faith, and was so healed. There was no way Jesus could have felt the touch to His clothes. He was being pressed and thronged by the crowd. Yet when she pressed her way and touched His clothes, she received exactly what she needed. And He will give you exactly what you need. As He is passing by, reach out and touch Him with praise and thanksgiving!

Jesus allowed this woman to be healed without embarrassment, but it was not enough to believe in secret. The secret disciple had to be brought to the point of confessing her faith. Your testimony of God's deliverance is not only for your benefit, but also for those who are behind you in the crowd; who are yet pressing their way through behind you. Sometimes after you're healed, there is a voice that tells you that you're not. That voice is trying to get you to doubt. That voice is seeking to overcome you. However, ". . . they overcame him by the blood of the Lamb, and by the word of their testimony . . ." (Revelation 12:11). You need faith to receive your healing, and you need faith to keep your healing. This is why it is so important to testify of your deliverance. Your testimony is for your benefit and those behind you.

We have people who were once in our midst who are like this woman, alone and lost. We have friends and family who are hurting, and who have been hurt and no longer attend our services. Sometimes we sin, then fall into self condemnation and quit coming to church. When we notice folks are missing we need to reach out to them and let them feel the touch of the Master's hand. We need to reach out in love to one another. "By this shall all men know that ye are my disciples, if ye have love one to another" (John 13:35). We need to reach out to those who have left our church and tell them that God loves them, and that they are missed. The service is not the same without them.

Satan loves it when a member quits coming to church. We are one body with many members. Our individual members make up the church. When a member quits coming to church, we lose the benefits of their talents and gifts. Satan loves it when a member quits coming to church and goes unnoticed, for when a member is absent, we can't benefit from their gifts and talents, and they can't benefit from what we have to offer. When the Lord appeared to the disciples after the resurrection, Thomas had missed the service, and he missed being in the presence of the Lord. The Lord didn't visit the disciples again until eight days later. It cost Thomas when he missed the service (John 20:24-29). Remember, "Not forsaking the assembling of ourselves together, as the manner of some is . . ." (Hebrews 10:25).

This woman was healed immediately, but there is another side of the coin. The Apostle Paul testified of a condition he had. Paul states, "And lest I should be exalted above measure through the abundance of the revelations, there was given to me a thorn in the flesh, the messenger of Satan to buffet me, lest I should be exalted above measure. For this thing I besought the Lord thrice, that it might depart from me. And he said unto me, My grace is sufficient for thee: for my strength is made perfect in weakness. Most gladly therefore will I rather glory in my infirmities, that the power of Christ may rest upon me. Therefore I take pleasure in infirmities, in reproaches, in necessities, in persecutions, in distresses for Christ's sake: for when I am weak, then am I strong. I am become a fool in glorying . . ." (2 Corinthians 12:7-11). Paul learned in everything to give thanks (1 Thessalonians 5:18).

Paul had a thorn in the flesh. It was an infirmity. It was an issue. Paul sought God three times for healing. The Lord answered Paul and said His grace was sufficient. Paul wanted to be delivered from it. But it was God's will that he live with it. God was saying that He was at His best when we are at our worst. When you're where you can't help God, then that is where He can get all the glory and praise. The thorn resulted in Paul praying and seeking God. And prayer is a good thing. Sometimes we can't pray when everything is going well.

But what Paul learned was that God's grace was sufficient and that His strength was made perfect in weakness. As a result Paul came to understand a very important principle. When you can learn to glory and praise God in your infirmities the power of God will rest upon you. Then Paul understood that he should not only praise God in his infirmities, but in reproaches, necessities, persecutions, and in distresses for Christ's sake: for when he is weak, Christ is strong. Paul went even further and said he actually became a fool in glorifying and praising God. Paul didn't take things to another level, he took it to another dimension!

You have to seek God for His will with regards to your specific condition. For Paul it was God's will that the issue remained. God said that His grace was sufficient. That meant it was enough. It was all Paul needed. Have you gotten to the point where God is all you need? Have you gotten to the point where in every state you are content? (Philippians 4:11).

Israel had to experience the wilderness for a reason. God was trying to teach them in their journey that He was all they needed. He was their cloud by day for protection, and fire by night to light the way. He was their water to drink when thirsty and bread to eat when hungry. Their shoes and clothes never wore out in 40 years, neither did their feet swell (Deuteronomy 29:5; Nehemiah 9:21). All they had to do was look to Him! All the disciples in the boat had to do, was to look to Him. The same is equally applicable to us!

Paul had learned some very important lessons, and lessons that we have yet to learn. In the 16th Chapter of the book of Acts, Paul had a vision: "And a vision appeared to Paul in the night; There stood a man of Macedonia, and prayed him, saying, Come over into Macedonia, and help us" (Acts 16:9). The Apostle Paul and Silas left Troas and went to Samothracia, Neapolis and ended up in Philippi which was the chief city of that part of Macedonia (Acts 16:8-12). While at Philippi, Paul and Silas were beaten and put in prison (Acts 16:22-23). In response to the beating and imprisonment, the scriptures state, ". . . at midnight Paul and Silas prayed, and sang praises unto God; and the prisoners heard them" (Acts 16:25). Paul and Silas' response to their issues and situation was prayer and thanksgiving (Acts 16:25). This is the example that has been left for us. This is important; sometimes our first response when mistreated is revenge. Sometimes folks devote their lives making folks miserable or in making folks pay because they have been hurt.

However, Jesus said, "But I say unto you, Love your enemies, bless them that curse you, do good to them that hate you, and pray for them which despitefully use you, and persecute you; that ye may be the children of your Father which is in heaven . . ." (Matthew 5:44-45). The Lord said to love your enemies, bless them that curse you, do good to them that hate you, and pray for them which despitefully use and persecute you, not for their benefit, but for your benefit, that ye may be the children of your Father, which is in heaven. It's for your benefit! It's to help you.

The scripture tells us to: "Recompense to no man evil for evil. Provide things honest in the sight of all men. If it be possible, as much as lieth in you, live peaceably with all men. Dearly beloved, avenge not yourselves, but rather give place unto wrath: for it is written, Vengeance is mine; I will repay, saith the Lord. Therefore if thine enemy hunger, feed him; if he thirst, give him drink: for in so doing thou shalt heap coals of fire on his head. Be not overcome of evil, but overcome evil with good" (Romans 12:17-21). "See that none render evil for evil unto any man; but ever follow that which is good, both among yourselves, and to all men" (1 Thessalonians 5:15).

While Paul was in prison in Philippi, he prayed and thanked his way right into the presence of God. That's why when the doors of the prison opened up he didn't try to run or leave. His body was in prison but his spirit was in the presence of God! Although Paul was beaten down and in shackles, in God's presence he found fullness of joy. In God's presence he found pleasures forevermore. God would have us to both live and walk in the Spirit. "If we live in the Spirit, let us also walk in the Spirit" (Galatians 5:25).

Thereafter, Paul and Silas left Philippi, and passed through Amphipolis and Apollonia, and made their way to Thessalonica. After Paul preached to the Thessalonians, he fled to Berea, Athens, and ended up in Corinth (Acts 17-18). While at Athens, Paul sent Timotheus back to Thessalonica to establish the church, and to comfort them concerning their faith (1 Thessalonians 3:1-2).

However, while in Corinth, Paul wrote the Thessalonians a letter. This letter is known today as First Thessalonians. Paul wrote this letter right after his experience in the Philippian prison. In this letter we see Paul's mindset. Paul told the Thessalonians to, "See that none render evil for evil unto any man; but ever follow that which is good, both among yourselves, and to all men. Rejoice evermore. Pray without ceasing. In every thing give thanks: for this is the will of God in Christ Jesus concerning you" (1Thessalonians 5:15-18). Paul had done all of this at Philippi! Paul practiced what he preached. Paul told Timothy, "Consider what I say; and the Lord give thee understanding in all things" (2 Timothy 2:7). Paul understood clearly the benefits of prayer and thanksgiving in suffering. Your attitude while you're dealing with your issues is important. You need to constantly be in prayer and thanksgiving. You need to press your way into, and linger in, the presence of the Lord.

As with Paul, not all are healed, because infirmities can teach us valuable lessons to help us in our walk of faith. David said, "It is good for me that I have been afflicted; that I might learn thy statutes" (Psalms 119:71). Paul states in Romans that, ". . . we glory in tribulations also; knowing that tribulation worketh patience; And patience, experience; and experience, hope: And hope maketh not ashamed; because the love of God is shed abroad in our hearts by the Holy Ghost which is given unto us" (Romans 5:3-5).

One day, ". . . God shall wipe away all tears from their eyes; and there shall be no more death, neither sorrow, nor crying, neither shall there be any more pain: for the former things are passed away" (Revelations 21:4). But it's going to take faith to get us there.

Chapter 5
Her Faith

But the woman fearing and trembling, knowing what was done in her, came and fell down before him, and told him all the truth. And he said unto her, Daughter, thy faith hath made thee whole; go in peace, and be whole of thy plague

Faith honors God and God always honors faith. This certain woman's faith touched Jesus. It is faith that touched Jesus. Faith will never go unnoticed or ignored by God. The woman confessed. She had approached Him being unclean and had not requested permission to touch Him. But she had still been healed. "But without faith it is impossible to please him: for he that cometh to God must believe that he is, and that he is a rewarder of them that diligently seek him" (Hebrew11:6).

Faith is so important in receiving from God. "And Jesus answering saith unto them, Have faith in God. For verily I say unto you, That whosoever shall say unto this mountain, Be thou removed, and be thou cast into the sea; and shall not doubt in his heart, but shall believe that those things which he saith shall come to pass; he shall have whatsoever he saith. Therefore I say unto you, What things soever ye desire, when ye pray, believe that ye receive them, and ye shall have them" (Mark 11:22-24).

Faith is so important in our walk. "For we walk by faith, not by sight" (2 Corinthians 5:7). And in the book of Hebrews we find, ". . . the just shall live by faith . . ." (Hebrews 10:38).

It is important to note that Jesus told Peter that the devil desired to sift him as wheat, but He had prayed for him that his faith failed not. "And the Lord said, Simon, Simon, behold, Satan hath desired to have you, that he may sift you as wheat: But I have prayed for thee, that thy faith fail not . . ." (Luke 22:31-32). The Lord prayed for Simon's faith! It was that important in order to withstand the attacks of the devil. "Above all, taking the shield of faith, wherewith ye shall be able to quench all the fiery darts of the wicked" (Ephesians 6:16).

Of Abraham it is stated, "And being not weak in faith, he considered not his own body now dead, when he was about an hundred years old, neither yet the deadness of Sarah's womb: He staggered not at the promise of God through unbelief; but was strong in faith, giving glory to God; And being fully persuaded, that what he had promised, he was able also to perform" (Romans 4:19-21). You have to be fully persuaded; what God has promised, He is able to do specifically for you! Faith is that important to our walk. God has promised us salvation, healing, and deliverance. We receive God's blessings through faith. Abraham did not doubt, but believed God was able to do the impossible. And God did! God is not a respecter of persons, but He is a respecter of faith.

When it comes to salvation, we are told, "For by grace are ye saved through faith; and that not of yourselves: it is the gift of God" (Ephesians 2:8). Salvation is through faith.

"And beside this, giving all diligence, add to your faith virtue . . ." (2 Peter 1:5). The foundation was faith. The first thing was faith.

Jesus is looking for faith! The scriptures state, "When Jesus saw their faith, he said unto the sick of the palsy, Son, thy sins be forgiven thee" (Mark 2:5). ". . . Nevertheless, when the Son of man cometh, shall he find faith on the earth?" (Luke 18:8).

"But the woman fearing and trembling, knowing what was done in her, came and fell down before him, and told him all the truth." Jesus put the spotlight on her. She wanted to slip away into the crowd. She didn't want the attention. She didn't want to make a public speech. The value of coming to Jesus is that He changes us on the inside. He takes our damaged lives and remakes them in His image.

This woman's touch had not healed her. She was made whole by faith. Jesus called her to correct her thinking. "For she said, If I may touch but his clothes, I shall be whole" (Mark 5:28). Jesus corrected her, ". . . thy faith has made thee whole . . ." (Mark 5:34) Faith can stop your issue of blood and halt Satan's attack in and on your life.

We come to Jesus one way, and we leave in a totally different way by faith. The scriptures declare, "Know ye not that the unrighteous shall not inherit the kingdom of God? Be not deceived: neither fornicators, nor idolaters, nor adulterers, nor effeminate, nor abusers of themselves with mankind, Nor thieves, nor covetous, nor drunkards, nor revilers, nor extortioners, shall inherit the kingdom of God. And such were some of you: but ye are washed, but ye are sanctified, but ye are justified in the name of the Lord Jesus, and by the Spirit of our God" (1Corinthians 6:9-11).

Right where you are you can make your way to Jesus and receive the healing you stand in need of. Remember, "Jesus Christ the same yesterday, and today, and for ever" (Hebrews 13:8).

The scriptures state, "And such were some of you." Sometimes we forget the way we were. The Lord will wash, sanctify, and justify you. What a difference one touch can make!

You will find that the things that happened to Israel were for our examples (1Corinthians10:6). "Now all these things happened unto them for examples: and they are written for our admonition . . ." (1 Corinthians 10:11). They were written for our instruction and warning.

We find in the book of Exodus, "So Moses brought Israel from the Red sea, and they went into the wilderness of Shur; and they went three days in the wilderness, and found no water. And when they came to Marah, they could not drink of the waters of Marah, for they were bitter: therefore the name of it was called Marah. And the people murmured against Moses, saying, What shall we drink? And he cried unto the Lord; and the Lord showed him a tree, which when he had cast into the waters, the waters were made sweet: there he made for them a statute and an ordinance, and there he proved them, And said, If thou wilt diligently hearken to the voice of the Lord thy God, and wilt do that which is right in his sight, and wilt give ear to his commandments, and keep all his statutes, I will put none of these diseases upon thee, which I have brought upon the Egyptians: for I am the Lord that healeth thee" (Exodus 15:22-26).

The Lord said again, "If thou wilt diligently hearken to the voice of the Lord thy God, and wilt do that which is right in his sight, and wilt give ear to his commandments, and keep all his statutes, I will put none of these diseases upon thee, which I have brought upon the Egyptians: for I am the Lord that healeth thee."

If you do what God says, He will do what He says. God is a God of His word. The Lord can heal you of every disease and every condition. It is the Lord that healeth! He is just a prayer away. He is waiting on you! The woman with the issue of blood had faith. She believed, and her faith made her whole. Your faith also will make you whole. Jesus said, "Daughter, thy faith hath made thee whole; go in peace, and be whole of thy plague."

This certain woman now could say after she was healed and sent on her way delivered and made whole, "Brethren, I count not myself to have apprehended: but this one thing I do, forgetting those things which are behind, and reaching forth unto those things which are before, I press toward the mark for the prize of the high calling of God in Christ Jesus" (Philippians 3:13-14).